Copyright © 2018 Pamala J. Vincent.
All rights reserved. No part of this book may be reproduced or utilized in any form or by any means, electronic or mechanical, including photocopying, recording, or by information storage and retrieval system, without written permission from the author.

Produced by BookCreate
Seattle, Washington USA

ISBN 978-1-64316-141-9

Printed in USA

Lessons From The Garden

Seeds of Daily Inspiration

PAMALA J. VINCENT

WHY I WROTE THIS BOOK

Rosie was her name. She lived next door on ten acres. Sometime before we met, she'd a stroke and wasn't expected to live more than 6-8 months. We were asked to take care of her during the hours her husband worked swing shift. She defied the doctors' predictions and we began an 18-year friendship.

I was a young mom with two small babies. I struggled to be the kind of parent I desired to be. Because children need to play outside, and we lived on a creek, my two were never allowed to be outside alone. While they played, I attempted my first flower garden.

I'm told Rosie was a prolific gardener in her day. Due to a stroke, she often could not remember to eat, or get dressed, but on good days she could name every flower in the garden and instructed me on how and where to plant them for success.

Rosie would sit in a lawn chair and watch me work. She was quick to tell me I was a wonderful mother. But she was also quick to let me know when I needed to parent or garden differently. Often times she jumped from parenting advice to planting advice. I would ask, "Are you talking about plants or parenting?" She would just shrug her shoulders and smile. Thus began my first Lessons in the Garden.

These Life Lessons in the Garden changed me. They were and remain quite valuable. She had a way of coming beside me and training me on how to get the most out of life. She many times said that when she died she wanted to be buried in my garden. Rosie's spirit lives. We buried her ashes under her favorite Lace Leaf maple tree in a heart shaped flower bed. It is my greatest wish that you too will find her teachings admonishing and inspiring to your heart.

There are 150 stories. This is book 1. I'd love to share them all with you. Look for the rest of the series here on Amazon.com

ISAIAH 58:11

THE LORD WILL GUIDE YOU ALWAYS;
HE WILL SATISFY YOUR NEEDS IN A SUN SCORCHED
LAND AND WILL STRENGTHEN YOUR FRAME.
YOU WILL BE LIKE A WELL-WATERED GARDEN,
LIKE A SPRING WHOSE WATERS NEVER FAIL.

~ DEDICATION ~

Dreamers need to dream, but along the way they need inspiration, first-readers, editors, content fodder, and cheerleaders. It is impossible to list all who have contributed to my writing dream.

These stories started with a lady named Rosie, the first rose of summer, and her husband, Ben deHaan who convinced me to write for our local paper, the East County Gazette, whom I partnered with for more than twelve years.

Thank you:

Antoinette Ellis, who taught me how to put on paper the words which have been loaned to me from heaven. And often reminding me, this gift was not for me, but was my responsibility to develop for others.

My daughter, Mother, Aunt, critique team and BoP, for always being available to edit and let me run ideas past them.

My husband, who continued to say, "Keep writing, I think you're on to something."

My father-in-law, who told me to be on the dock when my ship comes in.

My son for patiently walking me through how the 'pros' do it.

Thank you seems so little to give back for all that they have given; but Thank You.

Thank you all, for allowing my writing dreams to become a reality.

~ CONTENTS ~

1) Acts of Beauty   9
2) Balance Disorder   15
3) Be Patient   21
4) Blueberry Wisdom   27
5) The Training Bench…   31
6) Colors of My Heart   35
7) Complaining is a Choice...   41
8) Coram Deo   45
9) Christmas Clarity   49
10) Crow Cry   55
11) Embracing the Stillness   61
12) Un-encumbered Flight   65
13) Extra Refinement   71
14) Fading Splendor   75
15) Fertilizer or Manure?   79
16) Garden Prayers   83
17) Getting to Forgiveness Quicker   89
18) Glitter's Secret   95
19) Heartwood   99
20) Independence or Subjection?   105
21) Be On The Dock   109
22) Motion, Inertia and Friction   113
23) The Almost Life   117
24) Come Closer In   121

CHAPTER ONE

ACTS OF BEAUTY

Whose adorning let it not be that outward adorning of plaiting the hair, and of wearing of gold, or of putting on of apparel; But let it be the hidden man of the heart,...
~1 Peter 3:3

"Oh, there you are," my friend said as she made her way to my garden. "What do you do all day out here?"

She isn't a gardener or she would know the answer, "I'm writing. Can't you tell?"

"In the dirt?" she looked puzzled.

"No," I laughed, "this is where I come to think before I write."

"OK," she raised an eyebrow, as if she ought to call the authorities to have me locked up.

When life presses in on me, I spend more time in my garden. Once, while visiting the Chinese Gardens in Portland, OR, I was told that, the Chinese believe the more responsibility a leader has in their country the larger their garden is; believing the beauty of the garden re-focuses the soul.

Practicing this philosophy, I find the garden speaks powerfully to the inner places of my soul like nothing else can do. So, I garden often. I head to my garden to bring order to the chaos in my life. Somehow, contentment seeps through my body once I have dirt under my nails. Don't ask me what the connection is, it just is. When I crawl into bed, stooped over from weeding all day, I feel deeply satisfied.

I used to think I just liked flowers, but through the years I've realized it is much more than that. Beauty summons calmness in me. It might be the birth place for joy and connects me with my creator.

God instructs me within the canvas of my garden. His greatness can be seen through the expression of splendor when green leaves transform into pink spring blossoms and golden fall colors. And beauty matters to God.

Like the miraculous leaves turning sunlight to oxygen, we ought to find a way to transform our gift of beauty. We need to embrace beauty to ourselves and interpret it to others like the photosynthesis of the trees.

In this world today, we can no longer be spectators in the garden of our life; we must be co-creators of beauty. Majesty speaks in so many ways to inspire the gifts that exist in all of us.

If each one of us could do what we do best and then share it with others, imagine how amazing this world might be.

Perhaps beauty is as simple as a well-written narrative that spurs the reader to act in a positive way, an art piece refreshing the spirit, a song sung to comfort a heart, a well-tended garden that brings beauty into the eye or feeds a hungry family, a play that causes growth or gives an actor a voice.

Beauty might be an encouraging sermon, an honest mechanic, a sensitive doctor, a wise police officer, a note to a shut in, a smiling professional, an obedient teen, a cooperative bill collector or a friendly neighbor. It doesn't take great sums of money, or large quantities of time; but it does take a commitment to doing our best at whatever we have the gift to give.

Most of us miss our cues to participate. Spectators ignore cues and are often distracted by trivial tasks. When I started practicing 'paying attention', I began to notice I noticed more! It wasn't long before I learned to recognize the opportunities to inspire beauty.

One summer, I taught a young man who'd been struck by lightning and lived to tell about it. It was his goal to return to his regular classes, so he worked hard to catch up. On a particularly tough day, when his frustration reached a peak, he turned to me and said, "Sometimes I feel like I'm shattered glass!"

I said, "Good!" His mouth dropped open with disbelief at my words, so I continued, "I don't know about you but when I'm in a church and see stained glass windows, they inspire me in a way regular glass can't, and they are made up entirely of broken pieces of glass." His eyes welled-up and, although school still wasn't easy, he had a renewed fervor for the challenge ahead of him.

A teacher doing her 'real' job encourages her students to do their best. So it is with artists, poets, firemen, doctors, parents, mechanics, cashiers, grandparents, waitresses, trainers, bakers, window cleaners and the coffee makers.

As a writer, one of my goals is to point my readers to new ideas and new ways of thinking. Daily I ask myself, "How can I share beauty with others today?"

It is my hope that you will see beauty and perform 'acts of beauty' as gifts to others and embrace the beauty within you.

LESSONS FROM THE GARDEN: *Seeds of Daily Inspiration*

CHAPTER TWO

BALANCE DISORDER

"The thief comes only to steal and kill and destroy;
I have come that they may have life and have it to the full."
~John 10:10 (NIV)

"Your garden is beautiful. I always feel so peaceful here," my friend complimented. "Is there a technique I need to know so mine will feel the same?"

"I always say old gardens are more appealing than new gardens—the reason is what you see here. Old gardens are tried and tested, so plants have been moved around. I've had years to figure out what grows well where, and which plants off-set others. I know how tall foliage will be and how wide the shrubbery will grow. This knowledge brings a sense of balance to each bed individually and collectively."

Balance is an essential part of feeling peace for me. Some people have a strong need for balance and others are a bit more loosely woven. There are also seasons to balance in our lives. I used to desire the short-lived, superficial energy of chaos but, at my current age, I'm enjoying a more relaxed balance than when I was younger. But the key remains, without balance in my life, there's no rest in my soul.

We all know someone who brings a whirlwind of energy into a room when they enter. On the surface, they look like they are accomplishing great deeds, but at closer inspection their energy can be tipped in such a way that their perceived power leaves a wake of destruction trailing behind them. It seems there may be a lack of balance between energy and stillness.

Often, young people will allow the energy of emotions to rule; which can be a bit like watching a tail wag the dog, or a speeding locomotive being run by the caboose! Enthusiasm and passion can outweigh their thought-filled experiences creating counter-productive endeavors.

Attaining balance in life can reduce your stress, increase your joy, and improve your sleep, by restoring harmony between your mind, your body and your spirit. Any time the body, mind or spirit is out of balance, there are consequences. For instance: food, work, exercise, sleep, and play are all good things in moderation, but taken to an extreme where an imbalance is created, the consequences can be negative.

Living out of balance can give us a live-only-for-the-moment mentality obstructing our view for the future. I'm suggesting we live 'present' in the moment-to-moments of our lives.

Each one of us, individually, has a purpose for remaining, given by the giver of life; a job or influences that only we can complete; if we are out-of-balance in our own life, opportunities may walk right by us without our noticing or recognizing them.

Most people appreciate a need for balance in their lives, but very few actually attain it. It is human nature to take on too many tasks and responsibilities and then suffer with overwhelming, stress-related fatigue, illness, depression, and a life that feels like we can't get off the treadmill.

As school begins, many are just returning to their normal schedules after spending time on vacation. For some reason, most of us act as if a two-week vacation will rebalance the other fifty weeks of the year where we function at the speed of light.

Two years ago, while in Maui, my wristwatch stopped working. I had to live on vacation for two-weeks without knowing exactly what time it was. Most people would enjoy that, but I struggled with it for a few days until I embraced eating when I was hungry, sleeping when I was tired, and playing when it felt right. I had to work at being relaxed. I know this might sound weird, but I took it as a signal that I live my life 'too tight' on a schedule and I've never replaced the watch's batteries. In fact, the watch has remained on the bathroom counter as a reminder.

I'm not saying I've perfected relaxing, but I have embraced the process of finding balance in my life. And it is a process. I like undertaking many things in one day, checking off my to-do lists, and falling into bed at night exhausted but feeling much was accomplished. I still have days like this, but I no longer do this every day.

I've learned to simplify my life by cutting my schedule, cutting clutter (that must be maintained), setting priorities and saying "No" to things that do not have a positive impact in my life or that of others. I give back to my community, but it is one day a week and it's on my schedule. I have a time of day that 'normal' life begins and ends for me. I don't take phone calls or work before or during those times. I work hard at being organized. I almost never procrastinate because procrastination is double-stress for me. I work at a job that I love and could do for the rest of my life. And I play. I have to schedule my play time, but I play consistently, weekly, so I am not living my life waiting for vacation.

Keeping the balance in my mind, body and spirit allows me to be present in my own life. I'm learning to 'help' less which allows my family and friends to own their own life situations. Because I'm moving more slowly and can really pay attention, I'm learning to see what is rather than what I want things to be and there is great wisdom, truth and freedom in this new 'slowness'. Again, I'm not perfect at this, but like my garden, I'm trying and testing the things that work in my life to give me life—an abundant life that allows energy to give to others.

"So how do you know which plants should go where to create a balance?" my friend asked.

"I had a general idea because of the tags on the plants that tell me how tall they'll grow. Until I've actually planted them, they are the ones that tell me how tall they will get based on the conditions and if it works for them. I've had some not do well, until I moved them and then they exploded with growth. Sometimes they just need a little change . . . new surroundings or a new focus."

"Are you talking about plants or people?" she asked.

I just smiled.

CHAPTER THREE

BE PATIENT!

And not only so, but we glory in tribulations also:
knowing that tribulation worketh patience;
And patience, experience; and experience, hope...
~Romans 5:3-4

Some people when disillusioned with life clean, eat or practice a myriad of coping skills. I weed! I'm not sure I can convince my insurance company to pay for this diagnosis, but the self-inflicted therapy has created the most gorgeous garden!

I am an individual—unique at the least, complicated at best—and passionate about life and the people I meet. Some would call me ambitious, while others call me bossy. Some say I'm a strong listener, others might say I'm nosey.

Somewhere in-between truth and my unique perspective is my opinion of who I am to and in the world. I was once convinced that my great knowledge in gardening would be well-received by my husband. Following the ensuing argument, I stormed out with a machete to whack away at the brush growing beside the house. The positive side is that I found a small tree slowly choking to death under all the vines and rescued it. What once was thought of as a mess of weeds today has produced a 40-foot Maple tree that shades the back side of the house with its summer canopy.

The problem with myself and others is that we begin to accept the opinions of the world around us as to who we are. When we start to value what others think of us more than what we know to be true of ourselves, we take a stand on shifting-sand.

When I was younger, I had a great need to be accepted by people around me. I allowed those I admired and loved, as well as those who had no vested interest in my success or failure, to have a say in who I was becoming. Some of the comments were well thought through and seasoned with wisdom for my sake. And yet others I listened to came from a place of self-serving agendas or short-sightedness. Some opinions were critical and hurt, but others encouraged and inspired me.

Several events in my life mark changing points. Some of these events were catalysts producing beauty in me like the Lily of the Valley that grows in deep and difficult places. But each of these events, individually and collectively, shaped me into who I am today.

In my 20s I announced to the world that the party could start because I had arrived! I lived in a college apartment and didn't have a garden to tend—perhaps that's why I had no balance in my life!

LESSONS FROM THE GARDEN: *Seeds of Daily Inspiration*

In my 30s, busy at the business of babies, I asked myself, "Am I doing it right?" That was the year I gardened to be alone with my thoughts and to get a few minutes without the babies. I would put them to bed and water plants for a break.

In my early 40s I remember thinking, "I like me; bring on the world," and I planted bold, bright, contrasting flowers.

Later in my mid-forties, as the children left home, I asked, "Now what?" I was actually lost for a while. I remember finding, in the garden, a baby bird too soon out of its nest and I fussed and cried over it for hours commiserating with its mother. This was the year I threw myself into gardening and the flowerbeds. I nursed my childless spirit to satisfaction with flower babies and spent long hours grooming them to perfection.

And now, just a few years later, the children have gone, and returned, and gone again, and I have adopted new philosophies for my life: "Keep it simple" and the new adventuresome spirit that says, "Let's celebrate everything!" So, this year, the annual flowerbeds have all become perennials or have been changed to rock gardens and dry rock stream beds (which take no time to tend to). We've placed plastic and bark-dust in places I swore would never see the chips. Our gardening motto has changed from "Wow, what if we . . . ?" to "Let's do it once." And, "That's enough."

I'm at a time in life where I may or may not outlive the 25-year warranty on the house roof, the new decking material, the iron lawn furniture and the stepping stones on the walkway. I instead spend more time lying in the hammock savoring the moment, and preaching 'slow down' to those that think I have something to say.

I'm much more interested in sitting in the garden admiring it, and just enjoying the company of whoever happens to be there with me. As I leave my 50s, I feel a sense of completeness, contentment as I, like my experienced flowers, turn my face toward the sun and revel in my failures and successes.

Somehow, now approaching 60 years old, I'm gripped with an anticipation of greater things to come. Amazingly, the garden looks its best this year. The new plants aren't new; they've established themselves and are comfortable where they are. They've grown up and bloom with clarity.

Perhaps all these years my need to weed and plant when under duress has served me well. I've finally learned to do what great-grandpa said, "Be patient with yourself; it takes time to build a whole person."

LESSONS FROM THE GARDEN: *Seeds of Daily Inspiration*

CHAPTER FOUR

BLUEBERRY WISDOM

Life is 10% what happens to me and 90% of how I react to it.
~Charles R. Swindoll

I meant to trim them in April and then again in May, but the little suckers got away from me until mid-June. My husband's treasured blueberry bushes can be seen from our bedroom window which reminds me constantly that they need to be trimmed, watered, and picked. So, this morning, with him looking over my shoulder, I finally got a chance to trim them.

"Aren't you trimming too much," he asked protective of his bushes.

"No, I'm only cutting off sucker growth," I answered.

"How can you tell the difference," he asked, holding one of the long shoots I'd just cut off.

"The branches that grow straight up and are a lighter green are suckers. They rob the plant of its fruit producing."

"But this one has three berries on the end of it. Why did you cut it off?" He stood there holding the branch up to show me the fruit.

"That is a fake-producer. It's three feet long but there are only a couple leaves and three blueberries on it. All the life- giving energy is being used in that long cane rather than being sent to the berries. It will produce blueberries, but the fruit will be small and shriveled up." I could see him thinking about what I said as he turned the shoot over in his hands.

"When you see stuff like this, you see a parable for life don't you? That's where your stories come from, don't they?"

"Yes."

"OK, Mrs. Writer, what's the parable for this?" he teased, sitting down on the grass while I finished trimming the bushes.

"I should have cut these shoots out in April when they were new, pale green and easy to recognize, but the weather was bad, and I didn't want to put the extra effort into coming out here when it was wet. So, they took off and really grew. Not only did they rob energy from the fruit production, but once they got a good start, they began to adapt their appearance and became hard to distinguish between the real branches and the life-sucking fake ones. They even fooled you." I winked and continued, "I believe bad choices in our lives and some worldly influences are a lot like these suckers. If we don't cut it out of our life when it's new and more easily detectable, as it grows we will adapt to it and before long the sucker looks like it belongs as a part of us. And while transgressions try to imitate real growth it has such a destructive nature we don't even recognize that it is slowly sucking our life dry; so, if we produce any fruit, it will be small and shriveled up."

He thought about what I had said. "I'll never look at a blueberry bush the same way again," he laughed and shook his head.

"That's the idea," I smiled. "That's why I spend so much time in the garden. God talks to me in word pictures here. I also need time to slow down to think and I do it here. I need the meditation time to be able to recognize the fake-producing indulgences in my own life and vigorously cut them out before they rob from my own production. If I don't take time to be still here in the garden, I can miss sucker-sin in my soul which is much easier to cut out when it's small. For me, your blueberries are more than a serving of antioxidants atop our cereal; they serve as a constant reminder to be vigilant."

"I don't want to interrupt your contemplation time, so I think I'll follow your advice," he said, getting up off the grass and heading towards the barn. "I think I need to contemplate how rebellion can 'catch' me off guard if I'm not paying close attention."

"Oh yah," I laughed. "How will you do that?"

Placing his arm up to his head in a dramatic fashion, he said, "I must go fishing and see if there are any suckers that need removing from my river of life!"

CHAPTER FIVE

THE TRAINING BENCH . . .

> When the world says, "Give up,"
> Hope whispers, "Try it one more time."
> ~Author Unknown

Everyone needs one. It doesn't matter if it's fancy, with ornate railings, or if it's a cut off tree stump. Its only function should be to hold your weight for long periods of time. I'm on mine today—a bench. In fact, I'm so convinced we need to sit and contemplate our lives, that I have nine benches deliberately placed in various spots throughout the garden and woods.

It's that time of year. That time when I take a reflective inventory of myself, make changes and hope for positive outcomes. I love an often-used statement by Dr. Phil, that TV guru of wise sayings: "If you always do what you've always done, you'll always get what you always got." So, if I expect new results, I need to embrace new methods of acquiring my end goals.

Sometimes change needs our brawn, sometimes it needs our mental focus, but sometimes it can be as simple as implementing a new attitude. And some days we just need a little hope.

The dictionary defines hope as "the emotional state which promotes the belief in a positive outcome related to events and circumstances in one's life. It is the 'feeling that what we want ... Just might happen.'"

Here on one of the benches is where I take life inventories. I pray. I contemplate my responses to relationships. I set personal boundaries, eliminate waste in my life, catch the vision of life beyond earth, and ask God to forgive me for being other-than-heaven-minded. Today, I'm sitting here in silent expectation. I want to be that steward arriving in heaven to whom Christ says, "Well done good and faithful servant."

When I strip away all the wants and have-to's, what I really desire to be is the kind of person who inspires others to their best. I want to help reflect love and point the direction to the source of love. I want to be an equipper of the saints and a gap-stander for those who need a defender.

Some days I struggle to know if my life makes a difference. I don't want to make a New Year's resolution and have it dissolve before the end of the month. And so, I return here to my bench to ask for more faith, more hope, more patience, more understanding, and more wisdom on how to give away all that I've been given.

As a gardener, I practice hope when I plant seeds and bulbs.

There is an expectation that, although I don't see all that goes on beneath the dirt, the seeds will produce a garden when spring arrives. Perhaps I need a spirit of anticipation, and the faith to believe God is busy building what I cannot see.

It's here on the bench that I once saw a doe and her fawn. She allowed the little one to wander a bit closer to me under her watchful eye. Minutes later, she ushered him away. I always wondered if she knew I meant her no harm and that they were welcomed anytime. Although I've seen their tracks, I haven't seen them for a year or so.

Two weeks ago, I saw the same doe dead on the side of the road near our house. I cried to think she died on impact and then wondered what happened to her little one she'd shared with me more than a year ago.

This morning I was compelled to get up early and spend time on 'the bench'. It was cold, and as I bowed my head to pray, I was aware of fighting myself to avoid speeding through my alone time with Christ. As I finished and raised my bowed head, ten feet from me, stood a yearling buck. He studied me without fear as if he knew me, and I marveled at his little spiked horns. As I watched his breath in the cold, he broke our gaze, walked past me to eat the pears off the dwarf pear tree still hanging from its branches.

I'd like to think this little one found safety and comfort with us and returned to a familiar place. I'd like to think this is a metaphor for the rest of my life—that others would find safety here. I'd like to believe I've found faith, hope and love in my life along with the wisdom it takes to give it away.

CHAPTER SIX

THE COLORS OF MY HEART

"And the rocket's red glare, the bombs bursting in air,
Gave proof through the night that our flag was still there.
Oh, say does that star-spangled banner yet wave,
O'er the land of the free and the home of the brave!"

Admiring our newly erected American flag, I look over the garden area where it stands, and I am thankful. Our home is the place where family and friends gather for the 4th of July celebration. The concrete basketball court serves as an excellent 'staging' area for fireworks. Although the kids are finally old enough to use a match without supervision, they still return home to celebrate the holiday with us. While spreading out the festive tablecloth, and red, white and blue paper plates, my mind wanders to days when I was the one hoping Dad would let us set-off something more impressive than just a sparkler.

Back then, the 4th of July was the highlight of my summer. I was raised a military brat. War and saluting the flag was more than just something in a history book. There's something about the military that stays in your blood. You may leave the service, but the service never leaves you.

I remember standing for hours on a dock waiting for the U.S.S Kitty Hawk or Nimitz to pull into port and return my father from months of sea duty. I can still recall the smell of his sea bag and the sound in the middle of the night as we received over-seas calls from Hong Kong.

Because we lived in military housing, all the families left behind often waited together for news of the sailor's safety. We were close knit. These were the days of telephone party-lines and Dippity Doo! Every adult was respected as your parent and we called anyone over the age of sixteen Sir and Mam'. We took care of each other. New births, Easter dresses and loss of teeth were all recorded with a camera for Dad to see. It was tough. We missed them when they were overseas.

There was great anticipation as the long line of sailors in their blues or dress whites stood at attention manning the rails of the flight deck when they pulled into port. The war to us meant: every time a ship pulled out of port, it brought the reality this could be the last time we saw our fathers, sons, brothers, and husbands.

In the military, the 4th of July is celebrated almost as extensively as Christmas! The day was kicked off with a parade. My friends and I decorated our bikes with long streaming red, white, and blue ribbons. We clothes-pinned playing cards to the spokes of our wheels so they sounded like motorcycles. We were placed in line behind the honor guard with its huge American flag flying above our heads, and in front of the floats that carried war veterans. Once we arrived at the fairgrounds, we were met by Uncle Sam on stilts, bandstands and enough food to feed an entire platoon. There were games of strategy and games of luck, if you had a mind to play.

All the kids in the neighborhood would plan to meet at the corn on the cob booth at a certain time. We would then make the rounds playing games and eating until we couldn't move. The adults listened to bands, and generally got reacquainted. The highlight of the games was catching the greased pig!

We'd piled back into the cars to drive to the dock just as the sun was setting. Dad would put a blanket on the hood of the car and we would join the chorus of 'OH's' and 'AHH's' as the fireworks began. There are a lot of things the military does right, but when it comes to patriotism and fireworks, no one can out do the armed forces.

I was trained at 5 years old to stop instantly and face toward the flag while it was raised or lowered at the sound of reveille or taps. It didn't matter if you were in a rousing game of Red Rover, or a neighborhood sandlot baseball game you stopped, placed your hand over your heart and stood still for the entire song. What's more, you knew where the nearest flag flew and you knew all the words to the songs played.

I retired from the Navy life when my Dad did in 1974. It doesn't matter that I was never enlisted, I lived the military life. I had an ID card, knew what the PX was for and understood that if the MPs or SPs were after you, it was serious trouble. When Dad retired, we were thrown into civilian life and it scared me. At the local high school, no one called adults 'sir' or 'mam'. Kids my age talked back to teachers and no one scolded or grounded them. In the past 25 years, I've begun to believe that discipline, patriotism and honor had disappeared with the times.

This year several students were sent to Iraq with the Army. Prior to leaving, they were stationed at Fort Lewis in Washington. One student called to invite us to visit him on the base; what a nostalgic walk back in time. The buildings, distinctly military were the same color, size and shape I'd remembered. I'd never set foot on this base before, but I think the military only has one set of building plans for barracks! And I'm certain they buy their paint by the tons, because whether you are in Great Lakes, West Virginia, Hawaii, or Oakland, the colors are the same!

But more than just being familiar to my senses, the military way of life hasn't changed. It is comforting to know patriotism, honor, and pride in a job well done are still the mainstay taught to the young men and women we call soldiers. Salutes are still crisp, and uniforms are still worn with pride.

Because I attended some of the meetings for family members to help support soldiers as they go off to war, I can vouch for the strength that still remains constant in our troops and their families. Time has not tainted honor and tradition in our young men and women.

During a decade when we might take our precious freedoms for granted, it is encouraging to see our young people eager and willing to protect this land we call American. They still protect our way of life.

I sit in my garden preparing to share a meal with my family without the threat of being shot or bombed. I sleep at night without fear of being yanked out of my home and thrown into the streets. I worship in a church of my choice, and I participate in freely speaking my mind.

I hated it when my father was away at war. I sighed a relief when my husband just missed the age for the draft in the 70s. And I've never prayed so hard as I do now for my students. Fighting a war many miles from home is a young man I've filled with burgers and pasta salad, and helped with his high school math. Although I've never seen the ravages of war directly, I have seen its indirect results. Perhaps I am merely older now, and more aware of war's true costs.

The stars and stripes erected in the garden waves to me as if it were an old friend. It beckons me to slow down and cherish even the simplest moments; to pay attention to all I have, rather than to wait and notice it when it's gone. Her steadfast colors insist I utilize the power of prayer on behalf of our soldiers at war.

But mostly her bright red, white and blue colors, flying unencumbered over my yard announces patriotism is neither dead, nor forgotten. Our nation's song can still bring a lump in my throat and a tear to my eye. Our flag smiles from my garden to remind me that Heroes are not a thing of the past; they are this year dressed in desert fatigues. And if she could speak to our soldiers of war, past and present, she would be proud to say, "The land of the free and the home of the brave."

CHAPTER SEVEN

COMPLAINING IS A CHOICE . . .

"Be joyful always . . ." ~1 Thessalonians 5:16 (NIV)

It was one of those days! I'd already spent the morning swatting away those negative thoughts buzzing in my head like uninvited yellow jackets at a picnic. I had 'should do chores' to do but didn't feel like tackling them. I had 'want to do' items on my list but no real zest for following through with them. So, I found myself in the car with the window cracked open for my dog, the stereo and my favorite mocha with no thought to where I was going.

I'd awakened this way, as if I'd spent the night sucking lemons or as if my life had some horrible issue to deal with when I didn't. Nothing is 'wrong' with my life, yet this nasty indulgent cloud hung low on my head, depressing my attitude. I tried singing to the radio and sipping on my much-loved coffee. When I looked in the backseat, my trusty lab was all smiles as we drove with her nose to the wind just happy to be with me. I remember thinking, I need some of that happy lab spirit today---what is my problem?!

Somewhere along the way, I found myself pulling into a nursery. Plants seem to work a magic on me when nothing else will. I meandered among the aisles of primroses and snow crocus attempting to soothe my out-of-sorts spirit. I have a hard and fast rule about not spending money on plants until Mother's Day due to the unpredictable Oregon weather, but today (albeit WAY too early to start thinking of gardening), I decided to break my own rule.

In an instant, I was lifted out of my own dark indulgences and contemplated the combination of colors I'd take home. The funny thing is I don't even really like primroses, but the beautiful bursts of color after months of no planting, warmed my spirit. Pink and yellow, those are the colors I would take home to plant. And I did.

Now, I'm not sure if primroses carry spirit lifting magic, but by noon I was better. So much better, in fact, when I saw my neighbor and he asked, "What do you know that's new?" I was quick to proclaim, "The primroses are on sale."

"Let's go," he said; "I have a bad attitude today and need to get out of the house." I laughed and a few moments later, my friend, myself and my lab were in the car heading back to the nursery. While we were wandering the aisles, deciding on yet more purchases, my lab found someone to love on further down the row of daffodils. To my surprise, when the lady looked up at me, I realized it was an old friend from my first teaching job. I was delighted to see her all these years later. We greeted each other warmly, and I asked her, "What have you been up to these days?"

"I just came from a funeral," she said pointing at the flowers she'd chosen. "These are for the family."

"I'm sorry," I offered, feeling guilty that I'd been melancholy over nothing and said a quick prayer for the family that must be hurting over their loss.

"It was one of those funerals that inspires you to live better," she said.

"How so?" I asked.

"It's funny," she smiled. "She was 96 years old and all we ever heard about was how great her life was. She always talked about how much fun she had as a teenager with her friends and simple things they did together. I always just assumed she was poor since she would have been raised during the war. But today I learned from her family that she was a teenager in a relocation internment camp."

I was instantly ashamed of myself for allowing negativity to rule my mood that day. I've never experienced life in a concentration camp. I even pride myself on making good things out of bad, but NEVER have I been tested to that degree.

We said our good-byes, my neighbor and I purchased our flowers and drove home silently as we contemplated the nursery-store conversation. My heart and head were definitely in a different place as I planted the new batch of primroses. I don't think I'll ever look at these little spring beauties quite the same again. And hopefully, each time I choose to complain, I'll be wiser in what I allow to touch my heart and attitude.

CHAPTER EIGHT

CORAM DEO

"Do all things without complaining or questioning so that you may become blameless and pure."
~Philippians 2:14-15

Again, the cell phone in my pocket rang. For the fifth time today, I needed to stop my pruning and answer my electronic appendage. For the most part, my life is by demand quiet and orderly, but there are some days that I feel pulled in forty-five directions with only the ability to do twenty of the tasks well. Today is one of those days.

I finished the conversation, returned my make-life-easier-phone back into my pocket, left the garden and headed for the car to take care of yet another mini-crisis.

I'd love to brag that I handle all things in my life with righteous grace, a calm spirit and an eagerness to be all things to all people. But, I'd be misrepresenting myself—truthfully, I'd be lying and would chance being struck by lightning.

In my quiet times, I found the verse above that says I should do everything without complaining. I tried that. All I did was complain silently until I couldn't hold it in anymore and when a friend asked me how I was doing, the answer exploded out of me like a volcano erupting.

I began to search scripture and pray about how to go about an unpredictable, sometimes not so fun life without complaining and being a burden to others. I still want to be a hero to my friends, family and students, but I also want to be real. So, I Googled the word joy.

What I found was a site that listed Latin phrases and their meanings. For years, I've claimed Carpe Diem (seize the day) but today I found Coram Deo (in the presence of "God"). This phrase literally refers to something that takes place in the presence of, or before the face of, God.

To live Coram Deo is to live one's entire life in the presence of God, under the authority of God, to the glory of God. Seems to me, if I want to serve God His way, it's not enough to just complete the tasks He's given me, but rather to complete them cheerfully.

Doing all things without complaining is about being present with and for the glory of God. It's not about just bridling my tongue or reining in my thoughts, it's acting on the core truth I'd just found.

No more stuffing my feelings until they boil over.

Will I be perfect at this new step of growth? I doubt it—I know me, but clarity can bring wisdom. Like my garden, I'm being pruned for the future. Now, I have a better starting place than before. As I returned to the garden, I set my cell phone on the stone wall, feeling confident I can embrace Coram Deo and that I am much more prepared for the next interrupting opportunity.

LESSONS FROM THE GARDEN: *Seeds of Daily Inspiration*

CHAPTER NINE

CHRISTMAS CLARITY

"No one is useless in this world who lightens the burden of another."
~Charles Dickens

While the garden sleeps, the gardener cannot. It's cold out here in the garden today—the kind of cold that warns of possible snow, maybe even magical Christmas snow. The temperature makes my feet and hands ache. But I set about finishing my work despite the cold, knowing the warm house will feel even more welcoming when I'm done.

It's no secret to my family and friends that I love Christmas. I look forward to decorating, and cooking for everyone. I love cuddling on the couch with a warm mocha and the room lit only by Christmas tree lights. I can sit for hours with the dog beside me, the cat on my lap, cocooned in a heavy blanket, watching made-for-TV Christmas movies. I have my favorites and can't kick off the season without watching How the Grinch Stole Christmas and Charles Dickens' A Christmas Carol. Don't tell anyone, but my favorite rendition of the old classic by Dickens is by the Muppets!

As I rake the last of the semi-frozen leaves, I remember hearing a quote that shares the Christmas Carol theme, "What if we woke up tomorrow with only the things we'd thanked God for today? What would we have? How would our lives be different? Would we have missed some things?"

It's all too easy to complain about raking the leaves, until I realize, I have leaves to rake. How selfish of me to complain when others would quickly jump to enjoy my 'dilemma'. And last month, I complained about doing laundry, until the dryer broke and I had to do laundry at the Laundromat. I have a new appreciation for a dryer and being able to do laundry at home.

While I was in the store, the day after Halloween, I noticed the Christmas decorations were already up.

Sometimes we celebrate Christmas as a holiday of excesses. And we've all heard the sermons about keeping the real focus of Christmas, focused. So, the Grinch has long since been a hero of mine when he proposed, "Maybe Christmas doesn't come from a store. Maybe Christmas, he thought means a little bit more." (Dr. Seuss)

Sometimes, like the Scrooge in A Christmas Carol, we live our lives without thought for how our present lives give or take away from the life of our future. I shiver when I think of the Dicken's

Scrooge saying to the ghost of the future, "Are these the things that will be or are they the things of what might be?" Oh, I pray when I look back on my life, I find I didn't live life like the Grinch or the Scrooge.

Sometimes, we live our lives so focused on the past, the present passes us by and we miss our own lives. Maybe we should pray we all have an epiphany or an angel like George did in, It's a Wonderful Life. Remember when Clarence, George's angel, said, "You've been given a great gift, George: A chance to see what the world would be like without you. You see George; you've really had a wonderful life. Don't you see what a mistake it would be to just throw it away?"

"Strange, isn't it? Each man's life touches so many other lives. When he isn't around, he leaves an awful hole, doesn't he?"

(Clarence to George from It's a Wonderful Life).

Now that I've cleared the leaves from the flowerbed, I can place the nativity scene in front of the house. Carefully lifting the baby Jesus out of the box and laying him in the manger, I wonder what His mama felt that night so long ago. As if this were my own child, I stand over the 'crib' and only slightly understand how much she shared with us. As I struggle to let go of my own children to live their lives away from home, this little scene brings Christmas clarity to my heart.

I'm so thankful for the gift of ultimate love created to be given away to all of us. I'm thankful this little baby was born to fill the hearts of man. If we embrace the Christ of Christmas, we can celebrate the Merry of Merry Christmas!

As I settle in for the night, I ask myself again, "So . . . , what if I woke up today with only the things I had thanked God for yesterday? What would my life look like?"

LESSONS FROM THE GARDEN: *Seeds of Daily Inspiration*

LESSONS FROM THE GARDEN: *Seeds of Daily Inspiration*

CHAPTER TEN

CROW CRY

*May the God who gives endurance and encouragement
give you the same attitude of mind
toward each other that Christ Jesus had…*
~Romans 15:5

I am a bird lover. Usually I look forward to waking up to the robins' gentle morning songs. I smile and slowly stir enough to look through the window for the regulars. Then I stretch and roll over in an attempt to recapture some of the bed my black lab has strategically scooted me out of and doze back off to sleep.

"Caw, Caaaaaawwww!" Oh no! There it is again. My muscles tense and my hair stands up on the back of my neck. Pulling the pillow over my head with clenched fists, I complain to my husband, "Can't you make it go away?" I usually sleep in on Friday and Saturday mornings, but this time the crow had won. I was AWAKE.

Climbing out of bed, I pull on a light sweat shirt and my workout pants. My faithful companion is already barking at the huge black crow through the sliding glass door, impatient for me to put my shoes on. I barely slide the door open when she bolts outside, leaping from the porch into the yard in an attempt to catch the largest black crow I've ever seen. This event repeats itself every morning; the crow arrives, producing no winners or losers, but a rude start to my day.

As I head out for my walk, the crow flies ahead to the opening near the creek to preen, yelling at the top of its lungs. Perched on a perfect overhanging branch, the crow appears to initiate the beginning of the day's game designed to torment the dog!

The crow yells, the dog chases, the crow flies up the path just high enough not to be caught by my lab who is barking and leaping as if she could actually, really, one day, one time, catch the crow. This game continues up the trail and back to the garden until my dog lies in the grass panting with exhaustion.

I don't know exactly when the crow arrived, but its obnoxious caw grates on my nerves until I wish it would just move on. I try to think of ways to encourage the bird to move out. I complain daily about its dreadful voice and that the crow has chased the other song birds away. In short, I hate when the crow shows up and want it gone.

One day I was lamenting to a friend of mine about how this crow had shown up and ruined the joy and peace of the garden. My friend stood there looking around at the beauty of the newly groomed flowerbeds, the sunlight filtered through the trees and shook her head, "It's a bird. It has no power to ruin your anything—unless you let it." Then she climbed into the hammock under the trees for a nap. She slept quite blissfully in spite of the constant squawking of the crow.

All too often the world presses in on us and we struggle with discouragement, fear and depression. We regularly let a little obstacle that normally would be just an irritant, become a mountain too tall to climb. And then, the humans that we are waste valuable energy either trying to push the problem away, or pretend it isn't there.

I can frivolously spend my resources trying to find the easy way around life rather than face what really needs to be done for my own benefit. We, as humans, are much like water, frequently searching for the easiest path. We also let fear and negative people encroach on our lives until we are fully in their grasp and choking us. We need to learn to pay as little attention to distractions, negative energy and discouragement as possible in order to avoid taking ourselves out of the game of life.

As I continued weeding and trimming lost in my own thoughts, I realized I was missing the beauty the garden offered to me by focusing my thoughts on the crow. I had let a grating vocabulary of cawing reach inside of me like fingernails on a chalk board.

I did some research on crows and found they are believed to be incredibly smart, ferocious parents to their own, have a language embracing over thirty distinct sounds, mate for life, and are very territorial. They appear to have clan rituals that demonstrate they value each other.

This crow would land on the grass and the dog would chase it. Then I'd see the crow walk towards the dog until the dog would sprint away watching the crow over her shoulder. This would repeat back and forth across the yard. As I continued to watch the dog and the crow, it appeared on closer inspection that they were playing a game of tag!

We also discovered today that the constant yelling of the crow was a warning from a protective parent to stay away from the big fir tree. There was a fat baby crow sitting on the branches eight feet up from the ground but twelve feet below its nest. The baby had evidently been taking flying lessons and wasn't yet back in the safety of the nest.

I felt sorry for the baby crow oblivious to the danger that surrounded him, and I was empathetic to the parent bird yelling at the top of its lungs a warning for us to stay away and a 'you better get back home now' to its wayward child.

Now I felt bad about the methods I had contemplated for getting the crow to move on. There was a family growing in our fir trees. All of a sudden, I wasn't quite so eager to have them go, or quite so annoyed at all their yelling.

So, what changed? The crow still makes certain I'm awake with an ugly sound, and now the fledglings are learning the same song. With a new perspective, the only thing that changed is my attitude. Now, why didn't I think of that weeks ago when they first moved in?

LESSONS FROM THE GARDEN: *Seeds of Daily Inspiration*

CHAPTER ELEVEN

EMBRACING THE STILLNESS

"Seek peace and pursue it," ~Psalms 34:14

There's just something about the unspoiled white garden that draws me. Perhaps in the contrast of my daily life, it's the quiet. In fact, it's so quiet I swear I can actually hear the snowflakes hit the ground. Maybe it's this silent stillness that beckons me outside.

The fresh fallen snow has a way of making everything look pristine, innocent and unspoiled. You and I know that under the blanket of spotless snow lie blubs, plant-life and even weeds re-fueling for spring. It's a mystery how to be their best they must draw into themselves, rest, and re-group.

I was encouraging someone recently and was able to say, "Hang in there; you're going to survive this."

"How can you be sure?" they questioned me.

"I have one advantage that you don't. I have experiences that have taught me that this is a survivable circumstance. Be patient, you'll see."

In our fast-paced world, sitting still and being alone with ourselves can be a coveted commodity. When I was younger, I didn't like to be alone with my thoughts, mostly because there were things about myself that I didn't like. But I've noticed as I've worked on changing those flaws, I can embrace the stillness and walk away refreshed. I even take pleasure now in evaluating or re-evaluating how I'm doing in life.

Sometimes when the wind swirls the snow tumultuously, I'm reminded of the tough times I've weathered, and rather than being fearful, I embrace the opportunity to have an adventure. Those experiences teach me not to fear the storms that may come my way, and they've taught me to value the sunny days. Going through tough experiences has taught me the joy of making good things into even better things! And to value all that life has to offer.

Snowstorms will intrude in my life from time to time, and I'll remind myself these things will pass. Once I move through the storm, hopefully I'll have a survival story to share with someone else—to inspire them.

Sitting out here in the snow on the wall, imitating the hibernating tubers, I'm taking the time to rest, to draw into myself, and to turn my face up towards the snowflake-maker who is kissing my eyelids today with delicate snow.

I'm alone with Him. His faithful presence inspires me. It's been an entire year since I sat here evaluating my "who am I's" and my "where am I going" resolutions, and today I'm motivated to dream bigger dreams. With the help of His wisdom and these quiet alone chats, I, like my garden, have grown and it feels good.

In fact, I'd forgotten how good it feels to embrace the stillness.

CHAPTER TWELVE

UN-ENCUMBERED FLIGHT

> "No one, sir," she said.
> "Then neither do I condemn you," Jesus declared.
> "Go now and leave your life of sin."
> ~John 8:11

Snow crunches beneath my boots on my early morning walk. As I make my way down the path to the creek amid the heavy snow-laden trees, I hear a familiar scream from over-head and I smile. Shading my eyes from the glare of the sun, I spot the Red-tailed hawk that allows me to share his territory. His gliding is graceful and free. His eye-sight is keen, never missing a movement below. I move to open ground closer to the creek; he screams down a reminder that we share a secret only he and I know.

I have always admired the raptors of the air. As a young girl, I spent hours reading the stories of King Arthur and the Knights of the Round Table. The tales of their bravery and code of honor stirred the beginnings of integrity deep within my own soul. Peregrine falcons were used for hunting and held the noble rankings of their masters. It was then that I first fell in love with birds of prey.

This past summer, doing research in Walla Walla, I had the most unusual encounter with a goshawk. As I walked the grounds of the Whitman Mission, the hawk appeared to be following my friend and me. No matter where we strolled, the bird followed. Each time we moved from site to site retracing the historical recanting of the massacre, the bird flew to a place within a short distance of us. I've learned in my life to pay attention when things out of the ordinary happen. Leaving the national park, we noted that the goshawk left, flying away as well. When we questioned the Park Ranger, he told us the hawk had just shown up: he'd never seen it before today.

As the day continued, we found ourselves at a lecture on a Native American Reservation. The young people and the elders of the tribes described the difficulties of tribal life today. A well-spoken man in his forties, respected in his council, began to speak of his faith. He completed his testimony by playing a lute in the traditional ways of his ancestors. In a state of prayer, listening to the soothing sounds from the instrument, I closed my eyes to focus my thoughts. What happened then has changed me from who I was to who I am becoming.

Clearly, in my mind's eye, I saw a large white hawk fettered to the lower limb of a tree by leather thongs. Each time this powerful bird attempted to fly towards the sky, the leather straps held it fast against the branch. The continued efforts of the mighty bird never thwarted its attempts to be set free.

At last, with a mighty stroke of its wings, it cast off the fetters hindering its flight and soared heaven-ward. As the sound of the lute finished the song, the hawk dissolved into a wispy white cloud blending into the heavens. I'm certain this wasn't a paranormal event, but it did grab my attention.

I opened my eyes to a room full of people attentively listening to the rest of the lecture. I sat there convinced that I had been given a message for my life. I had been through a particularly rough year and yet the message was quite clear:

> "Cast off all that encumbers your flight
> and soar to the heights you are intended to."

I spent the next month re-evaluating the direction of my life, and systematically appraising the activities I give my time to. I set goals for my life, both short and long range and bravely purged everything that keeps me from success. It was as if I were the hawk breaking free from the leather fetters holding me flightless.

Getting rid of everything that hinders has proven both tedious and rewarding. It takes dedicated effort to go through everything in my life and a willingness to see the good, the bad, and the ugly of myself. I created a personal "mission statement" and let it serve as a measuring stick for every choice I made/make. I looked at my work, my finances, my stewardship of time, and relationships, then asked myself these questions:

- Will this matter ten years from now?

- Does this move me forward or backward to my goals?

- Am I building eternal wealth or immediate success?

- Is this a fetter or a feather?

Soon, I and many others will begin making New-Year's resolutions. This year the hawk's scream will remind me to put on more flight soaring feathers and to avoid the fetters in life that keep me from soaring to my fullest potential.

CHAPTER THIRTEEN

EXTRA REFINEMENT

> "I will teach you about the power of God;
> the ways of the Almighty I will not conceal.
> You have all seen this yourselves.
> Why then this meaningless talk?
> ~Job 27: 11-12

Some days the lessons learned in my garden are words of wisdom for others. Some days the lessons are inspiring, loving, warm and embracing. I like those lessons! But there are those times when the lessons are personal, intended specifically to smack me up-side the head and shout in my ear. Today is one of 'those' days!

It's spring in the Northwest—arriving a little earlier than we're use to—but none the less, it's spring! My neighbor and I visit our favorite local nursery eyeballing all the new plants and fruit trees. I spend the day trying to find an olive tree that can survive the northwest climate.

Prior to arriving at the nursery, I studied what makes virgin olive oil 'extra-virgin' and discovered it had nothing to do with the type of olive. It is instead the amount of pressure placed on the olive when they expel the oil. The more pressure exerted on the olive, the more purified and refined it is. That means any olive tree has the ability to produce healing oil if it can withstand the refining pressure.

I think it's uniquely special that Christ chose an olive tree to teach us about ourselves. Olive trees can't just be planted in the ground; they must be grafted onto a strong established tree base. This transplant creates a dependent relationship. The base can exist without the olive branch, but the olive branch must remain graphed onto the base to survive and thrive. Once the olives are harvested, the extra-virgin olive oil has the ability to help physically nurture the heart.

I don't know how purified I can become, or if I'll even be any good at being refined, but I desire to be. I need to stop wasting the energy on little irritants in order to appreciate the work being done in my life.

Life really is about choices, rarely easy, but always necessary.

CHAPTER FOURTEEN

FADING SPLENDOR

"The one who was dying blessed me;
I made the widow's heart sing."
~Job 29:13

As the fall season announces arrival with cold nights and warm days, I marvel at the radiant colors all around my garden. I love the vibrant, vivacious colors of the summer garden, but there is a striking richness in the plants and bushes displaying their stately colors in autumn.

During the early summer, these plants provide the backdrop for the glorious display of warm weather bloomers, but as fall approaches, these normally supportive actors begin to steal the show. As the annuals die and the perennials go to sleep, farmers harvest their crops, and children work hard at their studies in school. To the silent fanfare of changing seasons, these grand ladies quietly adorn the landscapes as they reach their experienced maturity.

One of my favorite "ladies" is a cranberry bush deserving of her position in the center of the flowerbed that points to our front door. She is the first green backdrop in the spring, the summer canvas that reflects the purples of the hydrangea, and the bugler of autumn in her fiery red dress. Although her exit from the garden is not permanent, she passes into a slumber that rejuvenates her spirit and inspires the others to their best! It is rare that death and dying are so valiantly embraced.

It is the older, more experienced plants that know best how to bow out with style. I pray that when my last days arrive here on earth, I embrace death with the dignity matching these valiant ladies!

LESSONS FROM THE GARDEN: *Seeds of Daily Inspiration*

CHAPTER FIFTEEN

FERTILIZER OR MANURE?

"I press on toward the goal for the prize of the upward call of God in Christ Jesus." (Wesley's notes: 3:14 Forgetting the things that are behind - Even that part of the race which is already run. And reaching forth unto - Literally, stretched out over the things that are before - Pursuing with the whole bent and vigor of my soul, perfect holiness and eternal glory. In Christ Jesus - The author and finisher of every good thing.) ~Philippians 3:14

"What is that horrible smell?" my friend asked covering up her nose.

Standing in the flowerbed blending the soil with my magic compost, I laughed, "That is what makes my flowers so vibrant!"

"What is it?" she complained.

"It's rotted fish guts, decayed compost and blood meal."

"How long will it smell so strong?" she asked, not really excited about taking my advice on this element of gardening.

"It will dissipate soon enough, maybe a week. It's funny, I don't even smell it any-more."

I remember the first time I was introduced to chicken manure. We lived next door to a man who added it every spring to his garden. He would buy it early and 'cure' it in his driveway, so it wouldn't be too 'hot' to place on the plants. He ALWAYS had the largest healthiest-looking garden on the street.

When he offered me some, I reluctantly spread it near my flowers. It wasn't long before I realized the blooms were the best they'd ever been. Now all these years later, I've not only become a religious user of natural high nitrogen fertilizer, but I even make my own to suit my specific needs in the flowerbeds.

But as often happens when I garden, God reaches down and teaches me something about life in my little sanctuary in the flowerbeds. Life may often throw manure at us, and at first we notice that it stinks. However, the longer we stand near the stench, the smell begins to dissipate until we don't even notice it any longer.

All of us, at some time or other, have become immune to the negative goings on in our lives. Before long, we can't see that we are settling for less than we want, or desire, or deserve. But here's the unique difference between plants and people. When people will stand still and claim, "I don't smell anything anymore," accepting their situations as their lot in life; plants seem to rise above the smell and use the manure to become their very best.

My father used to laugh about fish fertilizer and tell me that it works because the little plants can't stand the smell, so they grow tall quickly to get their heads away from it! Maybe we ought to embrace the same thinking and step away from the stench that may be growing in our lives! Perhaps the 'stink' can serve to inspire us to grow above what others may accept as tolerable or adequate. And if we are faithful to rise above, we can savor the sweet fragrance of success in our lives.

CHAPTER SIXTEEN

GARDEN PRAYERS

'In the Garden'
"I come to the garden alone
While the dew is still on the roses
And the voice I hear falling on my ear
The Son of God discloses.
And He walks with me, and He talks with me,
And He tells me I am His own;
And the joy we share as we tarry there,
None other has ever known."
~Composer C. Austin Miles

I spent the morning meandering. I often stroll aimlessly when I need to think. Meandering looks like you are doing nothing, or it looks like you are distracting yourself from doing anything. But I have learned that meandering has meaningful purpose for my life that I must not deny myself.

Before I built my garden, I studied several famous gardens of England, Monet's garden in Giverny, France, and the gardens of China and Japan. In these countries gardens are regarded as essential to the balance of life. Monet created his garden for the eyes, his painting and the senses.

The Japanese believe, "It is good to have an end to journey toward, but it is the journey that matters in the end." Their gardens are designed to provide a place for quiet reflection and contemplation. The statues, running water and tufted moss create a cascade of texture and visual enlightenment. The masterful Japanese designers carefully choose a visual focal point that delights the eyes and refreshes the soul, creating awareness of the passage of time. It is this philosophy that inspires me to allow my garden to have natural stopping places—never a straight path through it. There are places to sit, places that provide different perspectives of the garden and the area around it.

The Chinese designed private gardens to provide a "spiritual utopia" for people to come back to nature, to return to their inner hearts. Chinese private gardens are spiritual shelters --- a place closer to nature, closer to one's own heart, while far-away from their real social lives. One of the first things you might notice in the gardens of China is the absence of symmetry. While there is still today an urge to control and dominate nature in the West, the eastern philosophies encourage worship of nature without controlling it.

In ancient Babylon, sessions of justice were held out of doors, in rich men's parks. The Song of Solomon of the Bible is perhaps the most influential poem in garden literature. King Solomon's palace was elaborately created and was said that his gardens were wonderfully fair to look upon. In Jerusalem, there were great gardens just outside the walls for both trees and vegetables because manure (considered unclean) could not be put within the holy city, however rose-gardens were permitted within.

Religion has been one of the prime reasons for creating enclosed outdoor spaces for gardens. The Temple of Ashur was set amid planted trees in the fertile plains of Mesopotamia. In early civilizations, sacred gardens were used for sacramental purposes long before religious buildings were constructed. These gardens were marked with fences and walls and designated as sanctuaries for prayer. The inner courtyards of temples were often sacred gardens—places to pray, seeking inner guidance.

The Old Testament of the Bible has many references to gardens and the New Testament describes many times Christ chose to meet and pray with his followers within them. Man was created in the Garden of Eden and Christ prayed His prayer of commitment, " . . . not my will, but Yours . . . , " in the Garden of Gethsemane; and, He was buried and rose again from a tomb in a garden.

In my garden at home, I have two archways, one sits at the entrance and the other at the exit. The pathway splits and winds around a fountain along with side trails to show you different groupings and various themes but both end up at the same place. It's not a big garden, but it serves one purpose—to cause a pause. It invites me to sit, to smell, to allow my senses to travel far away from the pressures of the world.

With today's sped-up tempo of living, we commonly fail to meander, to sit quietly and contemplate our lives, our purposes. We all have an inner need to matter in the grand scheme of things and yet we generally go about living our lives unconsciously. Then we wonder why we feel so hurried, unfulfilled and need to escape. Or we end up burned-out or labeling it a mid-life crisis. Maybe one solution would be to build more gardens and sacred places that encourage us to be okay with being still.

CHAPTER SEVENTEEN

GETTING TO FORGIVENESS QUICKER

But with you there is forgiveness,
so that we can, with reverence, serve you.
~Psalm 130:4

Once in a while, in the early months of the year, the rain stops, and the sun show up. Happy neighbor children, eager to be outside, head down my driveway on their bikes. They prefer my driveway because it is long, and they can gather enough speed to allow them to catch air. The jump is only about 6 inches, but I'm sure it feels like flying! This year, the youngest has shed his training wheels joining the 'big kids' for this adventure. He has not as yet gone over the 'jump' but is eyeing it as if to build his courage.

That's not the only reason they show up. The children always stop to talk and without fail want to help me in the garden. I think what they really like is that I give them 'grown-up' jobs to do like pushing the wheelbarrow full of weeds to the compost pile and filling the birdfeeder on a step-ladder. I praise everything they do and always have a special treat for them when we're done.

This spring is no different. Seeing their eagerness to help, I assign tasks after pointing out to them places where the new plants will come up, and where the old bulbs will soon make an appearance, and I caution them that they can help but they must be careful of these sleeping bulbs.

The fairies I hide for their benefit are easy to spot now that the garden is bare. I usually take them down, clean them and replace them in new hiding spots in the early spring. They are old enough now (except for the youngest) to know the fairies aren't real and they volunteer to take them down for me, so I can take them inside. They smile a silent secret smile to each other knowing the delight they will have helping the littlest one find them in the spring, and I agree to let them carefully take them down from their present spots.

I was wrestling with a blackberry vine that had taken up residence in-and-around my wisteria and I should have paid more attention to my young helpers' efforts to retrieve the fairies, but I didn't. To my horror, in their attempts to avoid the daffodil bulbs, my eager young helpers had broken the fullest branch of a twelve-year-old dwarf Lace Leaf Maple tree. This type of tree grows so slowly that about four years of maturity had just been sheared off.

What do you do in a moment like that? Screaming won't change the situation. Being upset with children who were only happy to help in my garden and had no idea of the value of the little tree in comparison to the worth of a daffodil bulb wasn't going to help.

I also watched helplessly as my young helpers tried to be careful to avoid the rose bushes but, when the youngest lost his balance, he dropped his bike on my clematis tied to its trellis. Since this clematis grows on old wood, the once five-foot-vine is now six-inches tall. In the space of a few moments, two plants I had devoted a great deal of time and effort to have their growth considerably shortened. When I just stood there staring at the double-damage, one of the older boys said, "We're sorry, will it be o.k.; it looks like it is already dead." I couldn't even speak to let him know the error in his inexperienced thinking.

Moments later, calmly addressing the problem, my young helpers and I agreed on a 'new' rule: "No bikes in the garden." Then we heard their mom calling them in for the day. Once they had gone, I ran from flowerbed to flowerbed like a frantic mother comforting her wounded infants. In their enthusiasm and youth, even though they had been cautioned, my young gardeners had unintentionally tromped through my garden unaware that beneath the barren-looking ground were prized slumbering plants.

Like this lesson from the garden, I am learning that my choice to be involved with people on a daily basis will at times cause me pain. And at those times, my commitment to love people, like my hands-on desire to make my garden into its very best, means I must accept the painful stings of their unintentional trampling of my work.

If I am devoted to fertilizing growth in those around me then I will be held to a standard that may not always allow me the privilege of reacting to my hurt. If I am to continue my mission in life, then I must be faithful to turn the other cheek. When I am unfairly and/or unintentionally trampled, I must learn to rest in the place within me where there is no need to defend myself.

That day my young helpers left truly sorry; but that experience teaches me that I must learn to accept that there will be others who will come and go without an apology, or even an acknowledgement of the damage they leave in their mindless stomping. I could allow the anger to bubble within me but what would I accomplish?

Alone now in the garden, I gently remove the discarded branch of the Lace Leaf Maple and retie the uninjured branches of the clematis into their rightful places. I realize the destruction the children had inflicted was because they were children and did not have a mature gardener's understanding. They did not appreciate the tenderness of the bulbs below the surface or the distinct delicacy of the maple's growing patterns, because they have not tended every inch of the garden over the years as I have. They have not seen the garden at the many stages of growth that I have experienced.

It is normal when we are unintentionally or unconsciously hurt by others to react by striking back. When hurt happens, moving through the ache of the pain and spending less time analyzing it, can move me to the forgiveness part—quicker.

There are many opportunities to fail or succeed when dealing with people. So, daily I am faced with a choice; I realize—I can yell and scream, pout, defend myself, point fingers back at others' flaws and claim I am the victim—or I can get to forgiveness quicker. This kind of 'un-asked-for forgiveness' is a gift for the 'stomper'. I will give them the benefit of the doubt by choosing to forgive.

As my garden matures, I will continue to welcome the children and to smile at their eagerness to help. They remind me to love the roses in spite of the thorns.

CHAPTER EIGHTEEN

GLITTER'S SECRET

"So, I commend the enjoyment of life,
because nothing is better for a man under the sun than to eat and
drink and be glad. Then joy will accompany him in his work
all the days of the life God has given him under the sun."
~Ecclesiastes 8:15

I'm not sure when glitter became my favorite color, or when others' opinions of me stopped being of such great importance. The adventuresome side of my life has always been like the glitter I coveted the first time I saw Peter Pan sprinkle it on Wendy, enabling her to fly.

In childlike innocence, I dreamed I too could fly if I only just believed hard enough. I remember spending an entire Sunday afternoon jumping off a tall wooden box behind our house believing wholeheartedly that if I closed my eyes tight and could jump just a little higher each time that surely the next jump would set me free to fly over the neighborhood.

The year I joined the local Brownies, our leader shared incredible stories of magical fairies living among the prettiest flowers in the woods. I sat for hours believing if I sat still long enough, I would certainly see a woodland fairy.

When the rain would bring rainbows, I knew there was a pot of gold at the end of it. It didn't matter to me that I'd never seen it, I believed it was there.

Glitter, I'm certain, can take on many forms and shapes. In my life, glitter has been the certainty that when mixed with creativity, ordinary things became extraordinary: Clouds become God's chariots just for my viewing, flowers smile, lakes sparkle, the moon beckons brightly, and snow dances like diamonds falling to earth.

A well-loved scarf with glitter on it was the essential costume while I danced with my dog, certain she felt the magic too. The glitter-coated tiara transformed an old bed sheet wrapped around me into a ball gown fit for a princess. Hand-me-down tutus when sprinkled with glitter transformed me into the lead ballerina for the New York Ballet troupe. Plain pine trees came to life under Christmas glitter. Construction paper became gifts of the heart with the application of glitter. And cardboard became armor when glitter was applied to the aluminum foil that surrounded it.

Somewhere lost in the journeys of making a grown-up life, glitter escaped from my grasp. I don't think I meant to lose it. But in the day-to-day hustle of making a life it quietly slipped away.

The babies' arrivals signaled the return of glitter in my life, although I only smiled as I watched their fascination with the sparkly stuff. I enjoyed its presence again but somehow it had changed…or maybe I had. I had become a spectator and failed to indulge in glitter's magic.

Time has a way of marching on despite our pleading attempts to hold it back. I've tried negotiating with time, refusing to acknowledge it, resenting its intrusion, and even going through the motions of embracing it! Recently, at a time in my life when I'm supposed to be wearing purple, and relishing it, I instead rediscovered my glitter, and I've found it in the most amazing places.

This glitter isn't the sparkly kind in a craft cupboard; it's in the luxurious decadence of well-made chocolates, the beauty of my child's face as she found her first forever love, my son's accomplishments as he does what he has set out to do with his life, the welcome rhythm of a rainy day, and a favorite cup of tea. I hear glitter in the laughter of a true friend, a new global connection, a seasoned musical masterpiece and the sparkle reaches me from the well-trained sculptor.

My seasoned glitter makes food taste better, songs sweeter, days full of life and family and friends intensely essential. I find myself getting up earlier, so I won't miss a sunrise, the glitter of morning dew, or the opportunity to live out my life in a dazzling fashion.

Once unaware of the important role glitter plays in my life, I'm more mature now and I better understand its magical secret.

CHAPTER NINETEEN

HEARTWOOD

*Let us hold fast the confession of our hope without wavering,
for He who promised is faithful, and let us consider how to stimulate
one another to love and good deeds...*
~Hebrews 10:23-24a

There's an old cedar stump in our yard that bears the marks of long ago loggers who cut this giant down. But the tenacity of the tree has withstood weather, disease, flood and loggers. It stands today. It reseeded and is actively growing. The original tree was four feet in diameter, and the stump is now four feet tall with 80-foot branches growing out of it. I climbed up in it the other day to observe something I'd heard about from an old logger. I wanted to see the 'heartwood' of the tree.

Heartwood is the portion of a tree that sustains it from disease, fire, insects or falling timber. Any or all of these situations can penetrate into the center of the tree, begin decay and kill the tree. The heartwood is the center portion of the tree and is surrounded by sapwood. I learned that Redwoods, which have a dense heartwood, won't burn! But the most interesting fact I learned about heartwood is that it dies to itself to be affective in protecting the living sapwood that surrounds it and produces growth. Even trees with dead heartwood can live hundreds, even thousands of years after the heartwood dies. Heartwood has a mission, a sole purpose—to sustain the tree at any cost, even to itself.

This made me think about my mission on this earth. Since the good Lord still has me here, what is my sole function? But more importantly, the big cedar heartwood showed me that I must die to myself to allow the life-giving sap in me to continue serving! Dying to myself, I believe is an affair of my heart with the Lord that will ultimately give away more of me and give me more of Him than I ever imagined.

Since I have a mission in life, I need a mission statement and a handbook of sorts to direct my do's and don'ts. Mine may not be yours, but I found two Bible verses that speak clearly to my sole purpose.

From today forward, I'll aim to avoid not only others but my own attitudes that bring out less than my best. I refuse to be passive about my life, instead actively be involved in my own future. I'll do my best to avoid negative people, situations and choices that stagnate me or go backward in life. My intent is to surround myself with people who challenge me, who won't accept excuses, and become bold enough to learn from my mistakes to create a new future.

I need to avoid at all costs being unprepared. I need to assess the day to day projects of my life and make a plan to either fit activities in so I do them with my best energy or choose to say no to them. This will allow me to embrace unique opportunities that add living to my life even if I don't choose the path they point to, but to embrace the newness of it all.

I sense the need to return to the heartwood of my growth as a human being. Here is my list of 9 commandments:

1. Happiness is my choice regardless of my circumstances.

2. Energy from a pure source fills the soul, the eyes and the heart in such a way as to allow me to give it away to others.

3. Attitudes of positive people are contagious. I purpose to surround myself with contagious people and to pass on the 'can do' virus!

4. Righteousness is a pillar for others to lean on, not a weapon.

5. Tenacity is a state of holding strong when others can't or won't. I choose to lay down solid unshakeable beliefs that grow tenacious roots capable of standing strong in order to support others in my sphere of responsibility.

6. Worth is not determined by a crowd of witnesses but can be demonstrated to them. My value is judged by an audience of One—Jesus Christ.

7. Observant: Paying attention can sometimes seem to be a lost art. I purpose to reign in my pace in order to be conscious of the moments of my life.

8. Objective: I promised myself to learn to respond rather than to react—to think clearly apart from my first reaction before I make a judgment, thus providing fewer opportunities to have to retract my words. Practicing this one principal helps me to sleep better at night!

9. Difference: It has been said that only 2% of the world makes a real difference in their lifetime; I choose to be in this assembly.

Now that my goals are clear, I'll put this list on the bathroom mirror, so I start my day with a single-minded purpose. And like the old cedar, it will not matter what circumstances surround me or what challenges I face, I will continue to grow.

LESSONS FROM THE GARDEN: *Seeds of Daily Inspiration*

CHAPTER TWENTY

INDEPENDENCE OR SUBJECTION?

Have I not commanded you? Be strong and courageous.
Do not be terrified; do not be discouraged,
for the Lord your God will be with you everywhere.
~Joshua 1:9

Have you ever heard the saying a weed is just a misnamed flower? As a gardener, I love all types of flowers and am even a bit sympathetic to a few flowering weeds. I might consider letting certain weeds stay in the garden if they knew how to behave themselves.

Weeds by their very nature, take over—devastating everything in their path. They use up the life-giving water and sunlight, choking out the intended flora. Weeds produce an abundance of green growth deceptively masquerading as a budding blossom, when in truth the growth becomes deadly to the surrounding plants and produces only intermittent florets.

Words and their producers can be like these garden weeds. Negative words are weighty and can undermine others by stunting their growth and squashing spirits, while positive words and happy-hearted people actually inspire others to want to take the next step even when it is difficult, painful or a stretch in their abilities.

The odd thing is, I believe negative people really want to be positive, but often as they attempt to assert their independence, they grow instead like the weeds and can become victim to their own negative worldview.

So how does a weed-filled garden become an inspiring flowerbed and how does a negative person transform into a positive one? First there has to be a recognizing of why we aren't already a positive person. A person who is ruled by negativity is typically ruled by emotions rather than reason. They live by how they feel and we all know feelings can be fickle. A person ruled by negative emotions and temperaments demonstrates:

- Lack of maturity by reacting as a child to a situation.

- Lack of faith in Christ's ability to handle their life, so they foolishly attempt to manage it themselves.

- Passing judgment without understanding.

- A person's tool box is single focused, if it's all they know.

- An "It's all about me" philosophy may appear to give the person permission to destroy others' spirits and dreams.

- Thoughtless people can use emotions and tempers as weapons and walls to intimidate, control or push away others.

There's a false belief we are safe from others by not allowing them to get too close to us.

Acts of abusive and negativity can demonstrate a life lived without the rock-solid truths of scripture. A person can't measure if they are on track or off track so they often allow how they feel to run the show. This is a bit like allowing a train with a long line of boxcars to be run by the caboose. It can do the job for a little while, but it will soon burn out. Wouldn't it be better to be a person who wants to have an engine fully-equipped with the strength to pull the load?

In my garden, pretty or not, I pull the weeds out before they grow roots deep enough to destroy all that is beautiful. In my life, I'm thankful I can easily recognize some of the weeds and wipe them away. But I am ever watchful for new varieties of weeds that may establish themselves in areas that I don't notice. To be successful at keeping myself independent from these truth-slayers, I must spend a great deal more time in the garden with our true creator.

CHAPTER TWENTY-ONE

BE *ON* THE DOCK!

Genius is 1% inspiration, 99% perspiration.
~Thomas Edison

Yesterday, I watched a hawk flying back and forth across the valley at Jonspur Point. The hawk's flying strategy was very specific and intrigued me as I observed. Each time he flew against the wind, he worked hard beating his wings into the breeze to gain altitude. Then he would turn and fly with the wind, a more relaxing flight but remaining at the same height. When he arrived at the end of the valley, he would turn into the wind and use the resistance to gain altitude. Once again reaching the end of the valley, he turned around and coasted at the new higher altitude. It was only when he flew against the resistance that he gained altitude.

After a great deal of time watching this majestic bird, I realized he held the same secret the Johnny Jump Ups do—they both know how to embrace resistance. The Hawk uses friction to lift it higher into the sky and the Johnny Jump Ups refuse to be hindered by difficult growing conditions.

Have you ever noticed many of us are not living our best life? We have excuses that keep us lazy, unmotivated, fearful, and passionless---and we carry ourselves in a somewhat gloomy fashion. We often become satisfied with what is and allow 'good enough' to become the perennial in our lives. We'd rather sit around talking about 'when our ship comes in' than get up and find the dock. I wonder why? Are we lazy? Do we just not care? Do we not recognize the gifts in life we have yet to unwrap or are we afraid to embrace the unknown?

What if we acknowledged ahead of time that life in general will have resistance, friction, at times lousy soil and we may even get stepped on in the garden path? What if we were to throw away all forms of laziness, fear, sluggishness or whatever it is that interrupts living our best life and agreed to be okay with aspiring to a goal the attaining of which will be the hardest thing we've ever done?

What if we refused to be content resting in the valleys or coasting on the wind? What if we embraced failure and paused when it got tough rather than quitting? We could decline to be satisfied with perhaps a too low opinion of ourselves or the often-negative comments from those around us. If we focus our energy on attaining our own 'impossible' we might find it's not impossible at all and encourage others to mirror our efforts.

Not too long ago I made the negative, self-defeating comment to my father-in-law, "Yeah, one day when my ship comes in, I'll probably be at the mountains." I laughed, but he set down his coffee mug, took my hands and said, "No you won't, you be on the dock! You be there waiting even if you have to stay on the dock and never see the mountain. Be there!" He has since passed away, but his words live on in my heart. I intend to be there. And every time I want to quit, I hear his voice, "You be on that dock!"

CHAPTER TWENTY-TWO

MOTION, INERTIA AND FRICTION

"I do not understand what I do. For what I want to do I do not do, but what I hate I do." ~Romans 7:15 (NIV)

I have a love-hate relationship with my garden in January. I love to garden when the sun warms my back and it's too hot to wear long pants. In January, it is way too cold to garden, but it's also the time of year when some of the best future growth can be stimulated. Reluctantly, I drag out my warm clothes, my gloves, fur-lined boots and head for the garden.

The roses have already been pruned to allow for loss from freeze and will be cut lower in the spring. I don't pull my bulbs out of the ground, so only the fittest will survive. The annuals have been cleaned out and are next plantings' compost. It is the Wisteria, the Rose of Sharon, and the Clerodendron that I'm after today.

To stimulate growth in these three beauties, I shape them while they sleep. Each shaping is mindful of individual plants and takes place by either cutting them back, cutting out cluttered growth, hanging weights to create a new direction, or sometimes replanting them to a more productive spot. The Wisteria must be shown where to grow next or it will experience wild growth that takes over anything close enough for it to reach. The Rose of Sharon is cut to look like an open hand pointing toward the sky, and the middle growth that simply clutters and robs the bush is cut away. The Clerodendron is trimmed, freed of clutter and weighted with hanging fishing weights to give it the direction of my choosing.

Each of us, like my garden plants, has a choice to make: forward motion, stunted inertia, or embracing friction to stimulate growth. For a lot of us, inertia may look misleadingly safe. And, making no change can give the false illusion of feeling secure and comfortable but can become backward motion.

Internal clutter has a nasty way of keeping us distracted or deceitfully busy, in order to avoid growth, confrontations, or embracing the responsibilities that lead to our own joy and success.

Weighting branches to create pleasing designs is an ancient practice. Like the Clerodendron, when I aspire to grow in a direction that is unfamiliar, I align myself with those who are mastering whatever it is I seek to do or be. Like-minded people move my motion forward and help to unlock my inertia.

Friction can be, and often is, uncomfortable, painful, and scary.

We don't know what lies beyond the lesson or growth but it may also be the very thing that causes the greatest evolution in re-creating ourselves. I marvel at what my plants teach me.

Perhaps this year, we can adapt some winter gardening techniques in our own lives, commit to pruning old growth, cutting away clutter, and embracing the friction. It's likely the discomfort of the January air will develop strong growth in our lives.

As I shiver in the cold, preparing my garden for its best year ever, I make a mental list of the things that hinder me and to start doing what may move me forward to bloom to my very best!

CHAPTER TWENTY-THREE

THE ALMOST LIFE

"I press on toward the goal to win the prize
for which God has called me heavenward in Christ Jesus."
~Philippians 3:14

It has taken an act of my will to get me outside on this cold, crisp morning . . . and I'm surprised to see a rose still attempting to bloom. I love this rose bush. She grows the most gorgeous peach colored petals that when they bud out have the softest yellow hue. Today, somehow missing the hibernation cue, she has endeavored to produce one last bloom. Cold nights have stunted her progress. Frozen, the beautiful rose bud has opened just short of its potential fullness.

Standing Outside the Fire is a song title by Garth Brooks that has become a sort of mantra for living my life. I identify with the line:

"Life is not tried if it's merely survived standing outside the fire."

The 'almost' factor seems to exist in most of us in the same place where fear finds its toehold in our hearts. Fear, it appears, has many disguises like: worry, dread, anxiety, apprehension, suspicion, disquiet, timidity or dismay. These heart-captors can grow a life of their own until we are crippled into the 'almost' trap. We may have 'almost' made a change in our life for the better, but instead choose to play it safe. Or we did make a change in our life without thinking through the negative risks or the effect our actions might have on others.

I often hear the comment: I'm trying to figure out who I am. We try on personalities and lifestyles to fill the void that begs to be completed. We sacrifice our integrity, core truths, and honor in pursuit of short term joy and validation as people, while unknowingly allowing the enemy to plan his next attack on us.

Perhaps instead of asking who I am, we should look into the 'what factor.' What is it that I'm supposed to be or do to give back to mankind? I believe each of us has been knit together by our creator with one special gift and a job that only we can do. Each of us has been assigned the opportunity to bless the people in the circle of influence unique to them. Our job is not to live our lives to serve ourselves but to give to others the best of ourselves. Doesn't it seem that by finding out our 'what' we will discover our 'who'?

As a mentor, a teacher, a parent and a friend, it is painful to watch someone dear to my heart struggle to answer the question of 'who' and come up with an 'almost' life. I trust that when God spoke these words cited in John 10:10, "The thief comes only in order to steal and kill and destroy: I came that they may have and enjoy life, and have it in more abundance," he meant them for our good.

I know we often think that we are victims of our circumstances or that we just have 'bad' luck. It seems there is a thief, a traitor to our fullness of life, and we allow this enemy to win! What is the worst that could happen if we put to death an 'almost' life and passionately embraced a life of abundance by choice? If we step out in faith and become all we are intended to be, what will we find?

If we pursue the 'what' of our lives with zeal, the 'who we are' would be un-necessary to define as we live our lives in fullness. Then and only then, the 'who we are' search will be completed.

And what if our passions and our joys in life, really do come from a creator that has placed in front of us a pile of gifts purchased just for us and we fail to open them? Perhaps we should honor Christ by diving in and ripping open every gift intended for us.

Like the frozen rose in my garden, with the spring we all have a chance to live beyond a stunted 'almost' life. Let's become bold receivers of God's gifts. We can experience the 'wow', a newness, a rebirth and a life of abundance. Can you imagine what our hearts, our families, our friends, our work, our town, our world would look like?

CHAPTER TWENTY-FOUR

COME CLOSER IN

> Tremble and do not sin;
> when you are on your beds,
> search your hearts and be silent.
> Offer the sacrifices of the righteous
> and trust in the LORD
> ~Psalms 4:4-5

"Are the angels out yet," I heard a small voice say.

Looking up from where I was weeding, I could see the twins standing just outside the garden gate. The smaller of the girls, Kristen, was almost completely hidden behind her twin. Leslie is the bolder of the two. She's been here many times before and knows she doesn't need to stay outside the gate, but she waits for her sister's sake. Their golden blonde curls, huge blue eyes and gentle sprinkling of freckles make them look like cherubs. They are identical twins in every way except for their personalities.

Leslie is interested in everything around her and approaches life with an embracing 'What's next? Bring it on' attitude. Kristen often waits for Leslie before she will try anything, choosing foremost to be safe.

It was Leslie who first ventured beyond their property boundaries, running through the trails in the woods that border my garden. She asked me one day why I had built my garden. I shared with her that this is where I come when I need to think or if I have a problem and I need to pray. I told her about the times I spent in my grandmother's garden when I was younger and how I loved the smell of the old roses. I also shared with her my favorite stories of Thumbelina and The Secret Garden. In wide-eyed innocence, she asked if she could come and think in my garden too. I often find her sitting under the arbor talking or singing to herself or to my cat.

One day while having lunch with a friend, we found several beautiful four-inch tall life-like plastic angels. I hung them up in the garden in places that, if you look carefully, you will find them. Leslie enjoys searching for the garden angels and today she brought her sister to help look for them.

Kristen, being timid, is not sure she wants to come inside the garden and I try to assure her that it's fine to enter and search for the angels. Leslie whispers to me that Kristen is afraid the angels are magic, and Kristen is afraid of magic.

Leslie bolts from flower-bed to flower-bed to quickly examine the places where she has found the angels in the past: inside the Lace Leaf Maple, under the Blue Cadet Hosta, sitting on a rose stalk, or next to the pond. Kristen stays put at the entrance even when Leslie finds an angel and calls to Kristen to come and see.

"I found one; it's the angel with the pink dress, come and see!" Leslie calls to her.

"I'll look from here," Kristen calls back to her sister, still holding tight to the metal arch at the entrance. Standing tiptoe on the rock wall, she struggles to see what Leslie is talking about.

"You won't really be able to see them well," Leslie answers back to her reluctant sibling, "unless you come closer in!"

"I'm afraid to see them," Kristen admits to her adventurous sister.

"But you're missing it. Please, come closer in," Leslie insistently attempts to get her to move from her safe place.

I sit quietly watching and wondering if Kristen will leave her sentinel post at the garden gate and experience the 'magic' of the garden angels. The difference between their personalities is opposite enough to keep a teeter-totter balanced.

From my spot in the weeds on my knees, I think of life and people in general. There really are two kinds of personalities: those who experience life with all the gusto of a wildfire and those who 'play it safe'.

I identify with both Leslie and Kristen's spirits. I used to be so shy that I was timid about everything. I was afraid of making a mistake and I was afraid I would not know what to do if a situation was difficult. I lacked confidence to 'try'. I used to worry more about what others would think of me rather than what I thought of me. And I'm not sure how old I was when I got the idea that taking a risk was a bad idea?

I believe today, that life is for living to the absolute fullest I can experience. I've made mistakes but as long as I learn from them they aren't really mistakes. I've risked and benefited from doing so. I am not guilty of 'missing out'. And I am no longer shy!

To remain overly-cautious, under the belief that I am in control of the world and stayed timid, I would be in danger of giving my power away—never experiencing life to its fullest. That's not the kind of life I want to live. I chose instead to become all that I can be.

Like Leslie, I am willing to risk, to try and fail, to move out of my comfort zone, and to attempt new endeavors. I'm ready to unwrap the gifts life wants to give me and turn my sails into the wind. I choose to live life as if I'm leaving it tomorrow. I am thankful I heard the promise in the voice that also said to me, "Come closer in!"

LESSONS FROM THE GARDEN: *Seeds of Daily Inspiration*

This is the first in a series of five books. These long awaited stories are now becoming available to more than just her family and friends. Return often to read the others for: New Parents, Teachers, Pet Owners, and the Holiday Edition.

Some of the lessons are:

Blueberry Wisdom

The Training Bench

Why Pathways should curve in the Garden

Embracing Stillness

The Almost Life

Be the Best You Can Be

Why Johnny Jump Ups jump up!

Complaining is a Choice

Coram Deo

Un-encumbered Flight

Back When: Back when I was growing up I lived with both grandparents. My grandmother was truely a powerful Spirit Woman of God (Chosen I call it now since I ended-up walking especially in her footprints.

However My grandfather bless his heart was a true Man of God Never Missed a Sunday in church

CPSIA information can be obtained
at www.ICGtesting.com
Printed in the USA
BVHW05s1103020818
523233BV00006B/13/P